AF251155

YOUR RIGHT TO BE DIFFERENT

by Roberta Bonnici

cartoons by Chuck Clore

NYD DISCOVERY BOOKS

Other DISCOVERY BOOKS:
I'm Scared to Witness by Roberta Bonnici (order number 02-0931)
Leader's Guide (order number 31-0820)
God, Me, and Thee by Marvin Gilbert (order number 02-0841)
Leader's Guide (order number 31-0821)

International Standard Book Number 0-88243-842-5
Printed in the United States of America
Order Number 02-0842

4

CONTENTS

A leader's guide (teaching and discussion) for use with this book is available from the Gospel Publishing House (order number 31-0823).

Introduction

You have just landed on a strange planet. You wonder what the inhabitants will be like. What strange powers do they possess? How will they respond to an intrusion by aliens from distant earth? You enter their world with apprehension to find:

A warm, friendly reception,

an absence of selfishness, violence, and war,

and a people who have no word for "hatred."

Sound too good to be true? Just a segment of "sci-fi" fantasy? Then read on. For this "strange planet" is really the kind of world Jesus was talking about when He spoke of the kingdom of God. That world already exists in the lives of those who acknowledge Him as King. Someday it will be the ONLY world.

In the meantime, He calls us to be part of His kingdom—to learn His ways and to give Him undivided loyalty. When we do, dramatic changes take place in our lives. We can never be the same, but are "new creatures"—different people than we were before.

That's what this book is about: your citizenship in the kingdom of God, and your RIGHT to be different by conforming to His ways rather than those of this world.

1. THREE WISHES

The rhythm of the tambourines and flutes became louder, faster, and more intense. All eyes were on the young girl who moved with the rhythm while brightly colored veils swirled around her. The rhythm built to a crescendo, then suddenly stopped. After a moment of breathless silence, the king and his guests broke into applause.

The king was pleased. So pleased that he decided to offer a gift. After all, it was his birthday. He could afford to be generous.

"I swear, you can have anything you wish," he told her. (Careful, King. An oath is strong language.)

"Anything?"

"Yes, anything."

The guests leaned forward, waiting to hear the young girl's wish. But no one, the king included, was prepared for her response.

"Give me the preacher's head on a platter."

Everyone gasped. What kind of killer instinct lurked in this little performer? Actually, it was her mother's idea.

What Means the Most to You?

John the Baptist was the new spokesman for God's value system, and that system declared that adultery was off limits. But King Herod had ignored God's rules and was living with his brother's wife. He thought a king could do as he pleased—until John reminded him that his actions were wrong in God's eyes.

Herodias, the woman in question, didn't want to be reminded. So she suggested that John be put in prison. That would keep him quiet! But even with John locked up, she wasn't satisfied. She wanted him COMPLETELY silenced. She saw her chance to do it by using her daughter.

Another time, another palace, another party, another king, and another queen.

This queen, too, had something on her mind. So she planned a banquet and invited the king. We don't know what she served for dinner, but it must have pleased his highness.

"What would you like to have?" he asked her. "Anything—up to half of the kingdom."

And do you know what she asked for?

A pair of water skis?

A stereo with a tape deck?

A new chariot with a sunroof and leopard-skin seat covers?

No.

She simply invited the king to dinner the next night. Dinner must have been a taste treat the second time, too, because the king repeated his offer.

"What would you like to have?" he asked. "Up to half the kingdom."

Now was the time to make her request.

"Let me live," she pleaded, "and my people."

Then the story tumbled out: the king's wicked adviser, Haman, had obtained permission to kill all the Jews, not knowing the queen herself was a Jew.

The king was furious when he heard what had happened. And Haman was scared. This dinner party also ended in death, but not at the queen's request. Haman had simply pulled one "me first" trick too many, and the evil he had intended for others came down on his own head. He was hanged on the gallows he had made for another.

What if you had a chance to be king? Sure, it would be fun

to sit on a throne and tell everyone what to do.
  And live in the palace.
    And wear the name brands.
      And ride in first-class chariots.
  But what about the responsibility? How would you make decisions for millions of people? And be sure they were the best decisions?
  Sound scary? It was for a young king named Solomon. He thought about it day and night. How should he lead God's people?

  Then one night he had a dream. It wasn't an ordinary dream. And we know for sure it wasn't from eating a deluxe pizza or watching a horror movie before going to bed! The Bible tells us God appeared to Solomon in this dream. And GOD, the Creator and Owner of the universe, gave Solomon a chance to make a wish!
  Solomon's wish could be unlimited, because God is unlimited. He didn't have to stop with "half the kingdom" or some other restriction. He could have ANYTHING in the universe, and all that he wanted.
  Just what WOULD a king want?
  The biggest, strongest army?
    The highest piles of gold, silver, and jewels?
      And a long life to enjoy it all?
  Most kings would. But not Solomon. His desires went

beyond these things. He was concerned about the welfare of others. And so he asked for WISDOM and KNOWLEDGE in order to lead his people.

Wisdom? You can't eat it, drink it, wear it, see it, or sell it. Sure, it's important to be smart, but what about the GOOD LIFE? Isn't that what kingship is all about? Solomon surely did shortchange himself!

Well, it didn't quite turn out that way. Because Solomon's wish was unselfish, God was pleased. And because He was pleased, He threw in some bonuses.

God said to Solomon: "Since this is your heart's desire and you have not asked for wealth, riches or honor, nor for the death of your enemies, and since you have not asked for a long life but for wisdom and knowledge to govern my people . . . , therefore wisdom and knowledge will be given you. And I will also give you wealth, riches and honor, such as no king who was before you ever had and none after you will have" (2 Chronicles 1:11,12, NIV).

A Value Is . . .

The Bible urges us to "seek . . . first the kingdom of God" (Matthew 6:33), and to "set [our] affection on things above, not on things on the earth" (Colossians 3:2). WHY?

Because what we love is what we really value.

And what we value is what we choose to do or be.

And our choices determine our direction in life.

They form our patterns of action.

To sum it up, a value is that which we cherish, choose, and act upon. It represents what is most important to us.

Where do we get our values? Psychologists say we pick them up from the people around us—our families, friends, teachers, and neighbors. We are shaped, even without knowing it, by our surroundings.

Everyone has values. The senior who just HAS to have that new sports car values possessions. The person who sees life as one continuous Disneyland values pleasure. The young lady who HAS to wear designer clothes and be seen with the "in" crowd values popularity and prestige.

God, however, has given us the power of choice. At any

time, we can shift gears and choose different values.

What values give meaning to the life of a Christian? We've already seen some of them in the lives of Esther and Solomon:

Love and respect for God,
    concern for others,
        a desire for wisdom and knowledge.

Perhaps you can think of other values you feel are important for a rewarding life. Keep in mind that a value is NOT a belief, an attitude, or an ideal. These do not become values until they are translated into ACTION. That's why Jesus said we must not only hear His words, but also DO what He says. So to discover what you REALLY value, take a close look at how you spend your time.

What Is Your Focus?

Many Christians say they value the Bible as God's Word, but can't find time to read it. Dave Creighton and his brother Jay found time, although it meant getting up before 5 o'clock each morning and studying for 2 hours before school. Their focus on Bible study made them national Bible quiz champions.

Christians also say they value people and missions. But nine young people in Saline, Michigan, proved it. They held car washes and bike-a-thons to raise money so they could spend a week ministering to American Indians in Arizona.

The truth is: When we REALLY value something, we find time for it. We focus our energies in the direction of our desires. And we see them come to fulfillment!

Take an honest look at how you spend your time. If you're not satisfied with what you discover, prepare to make some changes. The Holy Spirit is waiting to help you make God's values YOUR values.

If YOU could have three wishes, what would they be? Remember God's promise: "Delight yourself in the Lord and He will give you the desires of your heart" (Psalm 37:4, NIV).

DISCOVERY PROJECT: WHAT DO I VALUE?

List the following items in order of their importance to you, based on your interest and the amount of time spent in these areas. Add items that may not be on the list but apply to you.

1. Television	1. _Your friends (example)_
2. Family activities	2. _______________
3. Church	3. _______________
4. "Things" (Using them, earning them, wishing for them, caring for them.)	4. _______________
5. The Bible	5. _______________
6. Your friends	6. _______________
7. School activities	7. _______________
8. Study	8. _______________
9. Your appearance	9. _______________
10. Community projects	10. _______________
11. Witnessing	11. _______________
12. _______________	12. _______________
13. _______________	13. _______________
14. _______________	14. _______________

2. CONSIDER THE SOURCE

The landscape was harsh and bare. Rocks. Scrubby bushes. A hardened crust of earth. It could almost be a scene from another planet.

Signs of life were hard to find. Occasionally a lizard or a snake moved across a rock. Overhead, circling vultures waited for death to provide a meal.

Here in the lonely stillness the prophets had fasted, waiting to hear the voice of God. Now Another waited, fasting and praying, but oh so hungry!

Then He heard a voice. It offered a solution.

"You need not be hungry," the voice suggested. "If you are the Son of God, command the stones to be made bread."

The stones were hard and brittle, but He had the power. . . . He could almost see them changing to soft, brown crusty loaves. What good would He do the world if He starved to death?

"Save yourself," the voice seemed to be saying.

Suddenly Jesus recognized the source of that voice. It was His enemy, Satan, sounding concerned about His life. Actually, it was a temptation for Jesus to trust in His own power rather than in the Word of God.

To give in to His desires instead of His Father's will.

To use authority over nature to satisfy His own needs.

Jesus knew that voice, with its plea for self to be put first, and He said, "No."

The voice returned. How was Jesus going to get started in His ministry? If people saw something spectacular, they would believe.

"Throw yourself down from the top of the temple. The angels will come and rescue you."

What a miracle that would be! And right in the temple where everyone could see it! It would be proof that God had sent a deliverer. The people would accept Him then and there!

But Jesus knew that wasn't God's way. He was to be a servant, not exercising power over people or manipulating them with sensational performances, but meeting their needs.

Again He recognized the voice as out of line with the will of God. "Look Out for No. 1" and "How to Get Attention, Popularity, and Success in One Easy Plunge" were NOT in God's game plan.

If at first you don't succeed . . . , Satan must have thought. The voice was back, suggesting another action.

"All the kingdoms of the world. All their glory. All the power over them. You can have it! Power over people! Riches! You can do what you want with it. All you have to do is fall down and worship me. It will only take a minute, then it's all yours."

What an offer! Imagine being master over the entire world! And all He had to do was—worship SATAN?

Yes, Jesus knew that voice. It belonged to the one who wanted to rule His life through physical pleasure, instant success, and material gain. It offered Him a shortcut to the top, a way to have it all without the cross. Satan made his way sound so good, so reasonable. And so easy!

But Jesus knew He couldn't sidestep the cross. God would triumph, but in a different way than anyone could ever expect. And until the Father gave Him all things, Jesus would worship and serve Him only!

So Jesus stood His ground. He would not be bought by Satan's offers, so the devil backed off.

Whose Standard Will You Follow?

That voice still echoes in the world around us. The problem is that Satan is good at disguising his voice. He doesn't say, "Better watch out. This is Satan speaking." No, he is much too clever. He uses every trick imaginable to make evil look good, and to make good look less than desirable. He offers you a deal you can't refuse! But the purpose is sabotage.

The Christian's survival as a Christian in ANY human society depends on the ability to recognize and resist that voice.

A young Christian girl who had recently come to the United States from Ireland found herself alone and lonely in the big city of Philadelphia. She had missed her bus and was walking home from work when a car pulled up beside her.

"Want a ride?" a young man grinned.

The invitation seemed to offer excitement and diversion. Her Christian friends were far away. She hadn't even found a church yet. Here was someone who was at least being friendly. Why not accept his offer?

Then she saw the look in his eyes and realized the risk she was taking. Deliberately she turned away. "No, thank you," she said.

As she walked home, she gave herself a pep talk. "I didn't come to America to backslide, and I WON'T backslide!"

A few years later, she was on her way to Africa to be a missionary. The greatest adventure of her life was just beginning. She had no regrets for setting her standards high and obeying the quiet inner voice of the Holy Spirit.

To make the right choices, you must know the options. Take a look at our society. A democracy gives people the freedom to set the patterns they wish. In many ways that's good, but it means there can be more than one value system. Not every life-style is Christian. You must be alert and aware—and able to sort out what is acceptable and what is in conflict with God's Word. And THAT'S not an easy job!

Many different philosophies influence the thinking of people in our society. Get ready to add some big words to your vocabulary!

1. *Pragmatism,* or the *Utilitarian Ethic.* This system says, "Is it useful? Will it work?" The end justifies the means. Rules may be bent in order to achieve a goal.

2. *Hedonism.* Pleasure and happiness are the ultimate good. "If it feels good, do it," and "I obey God so I can go to

heaven," both reflect this thinking.

3. *Relativism.* This system believes that moral standards may change from one culture to the next. "Right" is determined by where you are and what's acceptable there. "When in Rome, do as the Romans do."

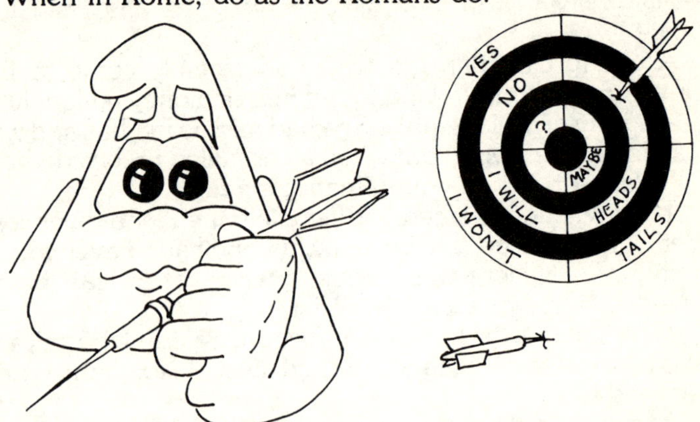

4. *Situation Ethics.* The situation determines the action. Whatever is the most loving thing in the situation is the right and good thing.

5. *Social Ethics.* The greatest value is the survival of the society.

6. *Naturalistic Ethics.* This system makes no room for the supernatural. It's a "five senses only" approach to life.

7. *Existentialism.* The existentialist finds meaning in life by creating his or her own values as life demands. Only by determining one's own existence does a person gain more significance than animals or things.

A close examination of these theories reveals an important fact: they all make their own rules. THERE ARE NO ABSO-LUTES! They reflect the belief that man is his own master (also called secular humanism). They fail to acknowledge that GOD has the last word.

Sources of Influence

What ARE the values our society approves and promotes? We get some big hints by checking what comes across on the "tube," the transistor, the billboards, and the newsstand. These forms of communication (also known as mass media) reflect the thinking and desires of the general public.

Dr. William F. Fore, an authority in media communications, has listed the following as basic values promoted on behalf of our society:
1. Power (i.e., over others and over nature)
2. Wealth and property
3. Love of self
4. Immediate gratification of wants
5. Comforts

The mass media also tell us:
1. We are basically good.
2. Happiness is the chief end of life.
3. Happiness consists in getting material goods.

These values are not only expressed in television and advertising, but also in music, literature, politics, education, and even religion!

"What does that have to do with me?" you may ask. It simply lets us know that the majority of influences around us are moving 90 degrees off course in a direction programmed for destruction. The old satanic sabotage hasn't changed much since Jesus' day. Temptation still says, "Live for yourself. Get all you can, any way you can. If you're happy, what else matters?" We can't depend on our society to give us accurate readings for our spiritual journey.

Look in the Book

Have you ever explored an antique shop or leafed through a grandparent's photo album? You probably chuckled at the clothing styles, the stiff, formal poses, and the overstuffed furniture. Yes, things have changed, and you probably wouldn't want to be caught in a 19th-century time warp!

That's how some people feel about the Bible. "It's outdated," they say. "It's old-fashioned. Not for today." And yet, the Bible DOES have a message for us. You can't read the Bible without meeting God's standards at each turn of the page.

The Scriptures show us the way to TRUE happiness,

which is a by-product of being in right relationship with God. The Bible also puts material things in their proper place: subordinate to spiritual values and the worth of people.

It doesn't take long to see that our social setting is a different world from the Kingdom in which Jesus reigns. The standards and patterns for behavior are not the same.

So which voice are you going to follow? If you're a Christian, you belong to Christ and HE should have the final word on how you conduct your life.

NOT the hot new rock star,

NOT the TV commercials,

NOT the suggestions of the "crowd."

Before you accept the latest "in" thing, whether in music, dress, or life-style, weigh it with the values of the Kingdom—the Word of God.

That's what Jesus did.

THOUGHT QUESTIONS

1. What are the values of the kingdom of God? (Read Matthew 5:1-12.)

2. How can I demonstrate my loyalty to Jesus' values? (e.g., in giving? peacemaking? self-discipline? serving?)

3. MULTIPLE CHOICE

"I was here first!"

"No! I was here first," an angry voice responded.

"He was here first," the companions of the first man shouted.

"No, *he* was here first," the companions of the second man shouted.

"Move over! Your cattle can't have all the grass."

"But we were here first!"

Then the pushing began. Before you could say, "All cows eat grass," fists were flying and a riot was underway.

Abram was in his tent when he heard the commotion.

"They're at it again," he sighed. "Why can't my servants and Lot's servants live in peace?"

Abram pulled back the flap of his tent and stepped into the hot sun. Shading his eyes, he headed toward the group of fighting men.

"Stop!" he commanded. "Stop! Every one of you! Is this any way for God's people to act?"

Slowly the noise died down. Lot's servants picked themselves up and began herding their sheep to another pasture. It was all right for Abram to sound pious. He didn't have to try to find food for the hungry animals. The flocks and herds kept increasing, and there was only so much land.

Well, Abram DID understand the problem. Only too well! But there didn't seem to be an easy solution.

A, B, C, or All of the Above?

Have you ever had a problem like that? One that wouldn't go away, but kept getting bigger and harder to solve?

Abram knew that sooner or later he would have to do something. So after thinking, rethinking, weighing the pros and cons (and probably breaking up a few more fights!), he knew what he would have to do.

"I'll give Lot a choice," he decided. "He can have the best land if he wants it, and I'll go the other way."

It was a hard decision. Abram loved his nephew. But he also loved God, and he wanted to live in peace.

So Abram said to Lot, "Let's not have any quarreling between you and me, or between your herdsmen and mine, for we are brothers. Is not the whole land before you? Let's part company. If you go to the left, I'll go to the right; if you go to the right, I'll go to the left" (Genesis 13:8,9, NIV).

So Abram gave Lot first choice, although as leader of the clan he really didn't have to. The ball was now in Lot's hands. He had to decide. And what did he do?

First, let's look at what he DIDN'T do.

He DIDN'T consult the Lord.

He DIDN'T ask his uncle what he thought might be best.

He DIDN'T consider who his neighbors would be if he moved to the plain.

And he DIDN'T stop to weigh the full consequences of his

choice: how it would affect his future and that of his family.
No, he could see only

    green pastures,

        well-watered land,

            fat sheep and cattle.

So he fixed his greedy little eyes on the best land and said, "I'll take it!"

Why did Abram give him first choice? Wasn't Abram afraid of what might happen to his cattle?

NO! Because . . .

ABRAM TRUSTED GOD!

Faith in God is an important ingredient in any decision. What appears to be best may not be the best. What looks good, tastes good, feels good, and seems to satisfy may be a death trap. (Just ask someone who has tried to kick the drug or alcohol habit!)

Decisions involve more than simply weighing the pros and cons. For a Christian, a decision is based on Biblical values, what God thinks about it, how it will affect one spiritually, and how it will affect others.

Lot's decision was to have far-reaching effects on himself, on his possessions, and particularly on his family.

And what about Abram? By acting on his values (peacemaking and generosity), did he get the raw end of the deal? No, because once again God honored a selfless choice.

And the Lord said to Abram after Lot had parted from him, "Lift up your eyes from where you are and look north and south, east and west. All the land that you see I will give to you and your offspring forever. . . . Go, walk through the length and breadth of the land, for I am giving it to you" (Genesis 13:14,15,17, NIV).

That was GOD'S decision.

A Story of Choices

The scary thing about decisions is that we may have to live with them a long time. (Something to consider before buying that purple sweater with the orange stripes!)

Decisions also create chain reactions. The aftereffects of decisions force us to make further decisions. (Give the sweater to your color-blind brother, or sell it in a garage sale?)

After picking the best for himself, everything should have been rosy for Lot. Right?

Wrong! His troubles were only beginning. Sodom became so corrupt that God finally had to zero in on the area with His big guns. And Lot, who had become a resident, had to run for his life.

"Don't look back!" the angels warned. But Lot's wife couldn't resist one last look. Her decision was fatal. Lot and his two daughters moved on without her.

The final chapter of Lot's life is pretty dismal. His daughters had missed any opportunity to find decent husbands. They chose an immoral solution to that problem. The influence of Sodom had stained everyone—all because of Lot's choice.

Do you see why decisionmaking is so important and how it reflects personal values? One of the most powerful gifts God has given us is free will. Yet few people learn to use this gift responsibly. Most decisions are based on:

1. *"If I do it, I may get caught."* Granted, the fear of punishment can help you decide whether or not to steal a car, rob a bank, or raid the history teacher's record file! Yet the basic motive here is self-preservation. Living simply to "stay out of trouble" isn't exactly life in its fullness!

2. *"What's in it for me?"* This motive is hardly any better.

Self is still at the center. And others may be hurt when the decision serves only self-interest.

3. *"What does the group expect?"* While the opinions of friends are a powerful influence, we can't let them decide all the direction for our lives. Group expectations may not reflect God's expectations.

4. *"What should a law-abiding citizen do?"* While this sounds noble, history shows times when civic duty demanded action that was out of line with God's principles. Roman soldiers were "carrying out orders" when they threw Christians to the lions. Executioners in Hitler's prison camps were "doing their duty" by killing innocent Jews. As Christians, our decisions must be based on higher standards.

When It's Your Move

Take a look at the decisions you face. Some are easy. (Whether or not to buy your kid sister a boa constrictor for her birthday.) Others are hard. (Whether to study for that math test or go to a basketball game.) But you can't escape DECISIONS!

Rick, an avid golfer with high standing on the school's golf team, had to decide whether or not to give up golf in order to get a job to earn money for a summer missions trip. He finally decided he should get the job.

While his friends were playing golf, Rick was cleaning chicken coops. It wasn't a pleasant occupation! But when summer came, Rick was off to Panama on one of the greatest witnessing experiences of his life.

Most decisions aren't the "life or death" kind. But sooner or later we face the "biggies." Questions such as "What will my lifework be? Whom will I marry? Should I go to college?" can cause a lot of anxiety. Wouldn't it be easier if God just gave us computer printouts with EXACT instructions?

Well, He could do that, but remember: We are not robots; we are His children. God intends for us to GROW in our ability to make responsible decisions. And that means struggling with situations and learning to plan, dream, and act in agreement with God's Word.

God has promised to help us with decisions. The Holy

Spirit has come to guide us into truth (John 16:13). We are also promised the peace of God as a witness to right choices (Philippians 4:7). We may still make mistakes, but when we make God's values our values, the desire to please Him can carry us far in making the right choices.

Remember: You are the sum of your choices. A value is what you CHOOSE to do or to become.

DISCOVERY PROJECT: Steps in Decisionmaking
1. What is the decision I must make? What are the choices I have?
2. What is important to me? What do I want to do or to achieve?
3. What do I know about the situation? What are the pros and cons?
4. How will my choices affect people near me?
5. What are the risks in the different choices?
6. What would be pleasing to the Lord?
7. What is my plan of action?

4. YOUR RIGHT TO BE DIFFERENT

"Kid brothers are such a pain!" Levi snorted.

"Seventeen years old and he's talking about ruling over us! Who does he think he is?" Simeon exploded.

"Well, I'm sick of his dreams!" Zebulun added.

For once, the 10 older sons of Jacob seemed to be in agreement. They all hated their younger brother Joseph.

And what had Joseph done to deserve all this ill will?

Well . . . uh . . . nothing. Somehow, Joseph was different.

For one thing, Jacob, their father, had given Joseph a robe woven with rich colors and pieces of fancy cloth—the kind that princes wore.

"Father never gave ME a special robe," Issachar sniffed.

"Nor me!" Naphtali responded.

"Nor me!" Dan chimed in.

Then there was the matter of the dreams. Joseph had dreamed his brothers would bow down to him. And he had had the nerve to tell them about it! Worse yet, Jacob didn't even correct him. In fact, he seemed to pay attention to what Joseph said!

"Look!" Judah pointed across the fields. "Here comes the dreamer now."

"Let's kill him and throw him in a pit," Simeon suggested. "We could say that a wild beast ate him. That will take care of his dreams."

It sounded like a good idea—to everyone but Reuben.

"Don't kill him," Reuben said. "Just throw him in this pit."

"Kill him!"

"Spare him!"

Back and forth the brothers argued—until Reuben finally won.

Is Everybody Doing It?

Before we cheer Reuben for being a hero, keep in mind that he was the eldest. He would be held responsible if anything happened to Joseph. His actions were based on fear more than anything else. So while everyone was in favor of killing Joseph, Reuben pleaded for his life, secretly planning to rescue Joseph later and return him to Jacob. He had good intentions, but. . . .

As soon as Reuben's back was turned, a caravan came by, headed for Egypt.

"Let's make some money," Judah said. "Let's sell Joseph instead of killing him." A roar of approval went up.

While Joseph's cries faded in the distance, the brothers divided the coins. When Reuben came back and looked in the pit, he was horrified to find it empty.

Well, if I had been there . . . , you may be thinking. Maybe I've felt like selling a younger brother or sister, but I wouldn't really do it.

Of course not! There are many things we would never think of doing IF someone else didn't suggest it,
promote it,
insist on it,
and make YOU feel like a perfect idiot for ever thinking of doing anything different!!
Sound familiar?

Reuben knew they would all eventually regret what they had done. Although they hadn't actually killed Joseph, he was "dead"—gone—as far as everyone was concerned. Now the problem was what to tell their father. Thinking fast, they dipped Joseph's coat in goat's blood and took it to Jacob.

"We found this. Is it your son's robe?"

Of course, Jacob recognized the coat, and his heart broke. Still, no one dared tell the truth or suggest going to find Joseph.

For the time being, "everyone was doing it." But down in his heart, Reuben knew that didn't make it right. Someday they would have to answer for what they had done to Joseph.

How Do You Cope With "The Crowd"?

What do you do when the actions of the crowd go against what you know is right? How do you cope? Here are some suggestions to help you make the right choice when your Christian values are at stake in a group setting.

1. *Know who you are.* As a Christian, your citizenship is in another Kingdom. You are actually a stranger in this world, on a peace mission for the King of kings.

You are normal (that is, you eat cereal for breakfast, read the comic section of the newspaper, and put off homework until the last possible minute), but you are not ordinary. There's a goodness in your life that wouldn't be there without a personal friendship with God's Son.

You belong to a special group of people—Christ's church. You live to reflect the majesty and dignity of the Ruler of the universe. You want to please Him. Your pattern for action is God's Word, not the influences around you.

You are confident and secure in God's love. He cared enough to die for you, and you know that NOTHING can separate you from that love.

Jesus knew the source of His identity and security. He didn't need the crowd to give Him status. You, as one of His followers, can have the same freedom to "be yourself."

2. *Know what you believe.* Christianity is more than a "good feeling." God's Word gives the basis for the Christian experience. Study it. Memorize it. Think about it throughout the day. Get to know God firsthand. Don't rely on rumors about Him!

Take a good look at your values. Are they really YOUR convictions, or simply those of your parents, pastor, or church group?

You can make Christian standards your own by:
Learning the patterns of action and attitude that are pleasing to God,
settling the basic issues in your own heart and mind,
and living in obedience to what you know is right.

When you know God's values and are firmly committed to them, you have an inner strength to cope with whatever life brings your way. You don't need "escapes," such as drugs, alcohol, sex, or other "pleasures."

3. *Learn to say NO!* NO can be one of the most powerful words in a Christian's vocabulary. It is part of your protection in "enemy" territory and more effective than a laser ray gun! Say it kindly, but with determination. It can:
Protect your reputation,
preserve your conscience,
and keep you out of all sorts of trouble!

Joseph wasn't in Egypt too long before his boss' wife tried to seduce him. Joseph knew adultery (a sexual relationship with someone else's husband or wife) was wrong, and he had a two-part plan to deal with the situation. He tried plan A: A firm refusal to betray his master and to sin against God. When plan A failed, Joseph put plan B into operation: He accelerated to "light speed" and converted to hyperspace, leaving his coat behind him! Although he still had to face a jail sentence because of this woman's lies, his heart was

clean before the Lord.

You can decide in advance what your answer will be when you're offered that first drink or first cigarette, or how you will deal with invitations to sexual experience before marriage. Under the pressure of conflicting influences you may be unable to determine what is best. So CHOOSE AHEAD OF TIME. And know where the exits are!

Those who are your real friends will respect you and your values—even if they disagree with you. But if you must stand alone, remember that the LORD stands with those who seek to please Him by right conduct.

What's the Difference?

How can you pick a Christian out of the crowd? Do they emit an eerie phosphorescent glow? Are they all whistling "The Old Rugged Cross"?

Jesus said there would be one way of knowing who the REAL believers are.

"All men will know that you are my disciples if you love one another" (John 13:35, NIV).

Christians are the ones "out in front" in service to God and others—whether they ever get gold medals (or honorable mention) for it or not. The love that keeps on giving is their trademark. It shines through kindness, friendliness, enthusiasm, sincerity, and concerned action.

Christians are also excited about Jesus and eager to share His love with others. The "difference" is the result of a close companionship with Him.

Jeff Wood, an honor student, basketball captain, and all-around leader in his high school, decided to let the "difference" show when he was a sophomore.

"I finally got serious with God," Jeff states, "and began to see the importance of sharing Christ."

Jeff organized a Christian basketball team, the "God Squad," and by the end of the season everyone in the school knew about the team and their Christian witness. From there, Jeff went on to organize a Christian fellowship group, reaching out to more of his fellow students.

It's not always easy to be different. Jesus himself experienced rejection, hatred, and even death for the "crime" of bringing God's love to people who didn't understand love. But there was no turning back, for love is God's unique way of expressing himself to the world. Then, He expressed it through Jesus. Now, He expresses it through us.

This love has a positive side (helping others, sharing the "good news") and a negative side (hating evil, putting distance between ourselves and practices that dishonor God). It calls for a commitment. There is no neutral territory.

The Living Bible puts it this way:

"Don't copy the behavior and customs of this world, but be a new and different person with a fresh newness in all you do and think. Then you will learn from your own experience how his ways will really satisfy you" (Romans 12:2).

Back to Joseph. What was the difference in his life? The Bible says, "The LORD was with Joseph." Our lives will also be different when we walk with God.

Never be ashamed of your testimony or the new world God has called you to represent. Your example could mean the difference between life and death for the very people who don't seem to understand.

THOUGHT QUESTIONS

1. Read about the life of Joseph in Genesis 39 and 40. How many raw deals did he get for being different? List them. How does Joseph remind you of Jesus?

2. How can a Christian be different without being weird or phony? Name one way you feel God wants you to be different.

5. FENCES & FREEDOMS

A large group of people waited at the foot of a mountain. Suddenly a streak of lightning sliced the sky. Thunder rumbled through the hills like the echo of an avalanche. A thick cloud rolled over the mountain, blocking the peak from view. Then the sound of a trumpet pierced the rumble of the thunder.

The people trembled. The mountain was on fire! Smoke rolled upward, and the ground began to vibrate. The people moved back, afraid of what might happen next.

What was the occasion? Another eruption of Mount St. Helens?

Actually, the event was more significant than that. The place was Mt. Sinai and GOD had come to speak to Moses about the rules that would govern the nation of Israel.

Rules that would affect every part of their lives.

Rules that would affect generations to come.

Rules that would mark them as GOD'S people.

It was an important day for the people of Israel—a day that would go down in history (Exodus 19 and 20)—and it was an important day for us.

Why Rules?

You don't live too long before you discover that the natural world operates on definite laws. Your stomach, for instance, must be dealt with regularly. Feed it or it growls! Your body also needs a certain amount of sleep, or you become a red-eyed zombie!

Science teachers are eager to tell us about other laws: the law of gravity (which keeps your cereal from floating out of the bowl), laws of physics (which explain why you shouldn't touch that "hot" wire), and laws of chemistry. (Mix sodium metal with water and see what happens!)

Yuck! Rules! you may be thinking. Couldn't we simply do as we please and not worry about nagging regulations?

Sure! Why not? That would be a great idea IF:

All people were genuine Christians,
   selfishness did not exist,
      and temptation could be stamped out.

Then there would be no problems. What a wonderful world it would be!

While that idea IS God's goal, we aren't there yet. To help us reach that goal, God has provided some guidelines—not because He's some big "spy in the sky," waiting to pounce on us when we fail, but to encourage us in the right direction as we grow.

Athletes recognize the importance of discipline and training. Steve Troglio, in preparing for the Triathlon, DAILY ran 10 miles, bicycled 60 miles, lifted weights, and maintained a strict diet! An athlete knows that's what it takes TO BE A WINNER!

Rules are valuable for another reason: They provide protection; they form boundaries. Can you imagine what traffic would be like without stoplights, yield signs, and warnings at railroad crossings? Tragedy can result when people ignore these signals.

When rivers or oceans leave their boundaries, we have floods, tidal waves, death, and desolation. Water is good and essential—in its place. Out of its place it can be totally destructive.

One important area God has hedged in with rules is sexual expression. Within marriage, physical expressions of love are right and beautiful. But "out of bounds" (e.g., living together, trial marriages, casual experimentation, prostitu-

tion), sex can be destructive, accounting for 250,000 illegitimate births in America annually, vast numbers of abortions, a near epidemic of veneral disease, and a host of hasty marriages that have a poor chance for survival.

The Path to Freedom

Rules, then, have benefits. They provide discipline that can lead to greater freedom and achievement. They also protect us from excess, imbalance, and needless suffering. They guide and guard us. Now let's look more closely at the intention behind the rules.

God's first command is that we love Him supremely and worship Him only. Is God on an ego trip? No! He is simply drawing our attention from lesser things to the highest and purest in the universe. There's a good reason, for WE BECOME LIKE WHAT WE WORSHIP.

When you admire a person, you try in every way to be like him or her. You may copy that person's hair or clothing style. You may even try to walk and talk like your "idol." You decide THAT'S the kind of person you want to be someday.

It's much the same when we truly love God. We desire to learn His ways so we can be like Him. As we learn what He is like (i.e., loving, just, righteous), we begin to find the pattern for what He wants us to be and to become.

With that understanding, we can go on to the second part of God's command: to love others as ourselves. THAT covers a lot of territory! "Me first" is NOT the rule in God's game. It's "You first."

The "You first" philosophy is based on the value system that says: Next to God, people are the most important part of the world. God not only declared the creation of humanity "very good," (Genesis 1:31), but He also gave His only Son to die so human failure could be forgiven (John 3:16). Since God has placed this high value on people, we are to do the same.

We see this principle at work in the New Testament. As far as "things" were concerned (such as food, clothing, houses, land), Jesus couldn't have cared less (Matthew 6:25). They were to *use*—not to accumulate or idolize.

But people? Now THAT was a different story! They were to be shown mercy, healed, treated with respect, and loved. And that was just how Jesus treated them. No wonder the crowds followed Him!

The Master Plan

Meanwhile, back at the mountain. What did the rules do for Israel? Through the discipline God gave His people in the wilderness, the nation that had begun as a group of runaway slaves became strong enough to survive thousands of years of "ups and downs" (mostly "downs"!). When the Jews lost everything—their land, their temple, their priesthood—they still had the laws of God. And that's what made them who they were!

We can learn a lot about God's value system by looking closely at the Ten Commandments. Jesus didn't discard the rules when He came; He made them more personal. They were not external laws to be kept, but inner motivation—a matter of the heart.

When we look at the life of Jesus, we see how the rules are supposed to work. They teach us HOW to love our neighbor as ourselves; HOW to avoid crushing and hurting others; HOW to put the concerns of others ahead of our own. In short, how to be like our Heavenly Father.

And so, it is wrong to dishonor parents, because it shows ingratitude for the gift of life they have given. (And in old age, no parent should be lonely or unwanted.)

Stealing is wrong, because it denies someone the right to

enjoy what God has given him or her.

Murder is wrong, because it destroys a person's chance to be what he or she could be.

Adultery is wrong, because it destroys the deepest kind of trust between two people.

Giving a false witness against someone is wrong, because it prevents justice from being done and actually protects the guilty party (while hurting the innocent!).

Coveting is wrong, because it focuses on THINGS, rather than on the needs of people. And when the coveting involves someone's husband or wife, it can lead to destroying a family.

Jesus said all these rules could be fulfilled by just one word: LOVE. That's what God's value system is all about. It's the LAW of the KINGDOM.

Sometimes people make the mistake of thinking the RULE is more important than the reason behind the rule. We call that "legalism." The Pharisees in Jesus' day were guilty of this. But Jesus set the record straight by showing how the rules were to operate. The commandments were just the *starting point* for a life of service to others.

If we look at the rules as interference, or God's way of spoiling our fun, we miss the whole point. They are intended to do just the opposite! Jesus pointed out that we find real satisfaction in life only when we give to the needs of others

(Luke 17:32, 33). The rules show us how. They are basic to our happiness—as individuals and as members of God's kingdom.

They are there to make us WINNERS!

DISCOVERY PROJECT: What Do the Rules Mean to Me?

Using Exodus 20:1-17 as a base, write your response to the question, "How does this apply to me?"

1. No other gods. _______________________________
2. No images. _______________________________
3. No taking God's name in vain. _______________________________
____
4. Keep the Sabbath holy. _______________________________
5. Honor father and mother. _______________________________
6. No murder. _______________________________
7. No adultery. _______________________________
8. No stealing. _______________________________
9. No false accusations. _______________________________
10. No coveting. _______________________________

6. LOVE IT & LIVE IT!

It was morning in Babylon, and Daniel's first thought was not orange juice and pancakes. It was—PRAYER!

Rising from his bed, Daniel stretched, then went to the window facing his homeland, Palestine. Dropping to his knees, he prayed.

"The Lord our God is one Lord. If I forget you, O Jerusalem, let my right hand forget its skill."

The people of Israel were in captivity. Although Daniel had lived in Babylon most of his life, he had determined as a young man to keep God's laws. Prayer was part of that commitment. So three times each day, Daniel knelt by his window and offered worship to God.

Servants in the courtyard must have looked up as Daniel's prayer drifted out on the morning air. Daniel didn't care. Let them hear him, and laugh, if they chose.

"Evening, morning, and noon I cry out . . . and He hears my voice," Daniel mused. "I will serve You and praise You, O God." Daniel could not forget his native land—or his God.

After his morning routine, Daniel set out for work. He was one of the king's three administrators, and he took his job seriously. He was never late, careless, or negligent. In fact, the king was considering appointing Daniel administrator over the whole kingdom!

What Daniel DIDN'T know was that the other administrators, a jealous green, had talked the king into making a law that could destroy Daniel. They knew Daniel's behavior was above reproach. In fact, he was TOO good. They also knew how much Daniel loved God. AND they knew how proud the king was.

So they mixed these three facts together and came up with a suggestion that the king outlaw prayer to any god but the king for 30 days, under penalty of becoming cat chow—for BIG cats!

The king agreed. He realized too late what he had done to his friend Daniel.

And what did Daniel do when he heard about the law? Demand his rights?

Picket the palace?

Take a quickie course in Advanced Lion Taming?

No. He did not change his schedule in the least. At the next appointed time, he went to his room, knelt facing the open window, prayed, and gave thanks before God—AS HE ALWAYS HAD DONE!

A Faith That Won't Quit!

Can you imagine someone WANTING to go to church? Not because parents insist,

or because there's nothing else to do,

or because of that new girl (or boy) who will be there, but because a person WANTS

to worship God,

to be with other Christians,

and to hear more about God's Word?

Daniel couldn't get to "church." Jerusalem was hundreds of miles away, and the temple was in ruins. But his heart was there, so he did the next best thing: he maintained his daily worship WHERE HE WAS, at the risk of his life, because he really loved God more than anything else in the world.

Some people see Christianity as a nice idea—for someone else to put into practice! But Daniel's beliefs were more than nice words and high ideals. They had become part of his life. They determined his behavior—even when he was away from home.

Have you ever felt like a roller coaster saint: up one minute and down the next? Be encouraged! All Christians experience low points and times of feeling less than "saintly." Teens especially are subject to shifting moods. By Monday morning, your Sunday night spiritual experience may be a faded memory!

Where do you get a faith that won't wear out, regardless of where you are,

who you're with,

and what's going on in the world around you?

Actually, three important areas must be cultivated if your faith is to produce a consistent pattern of action:

1. *The inner life of devotion* (that is, hanging around with God and showing Him that you care).

2. *The intellectual life of rational thought* (learning the basics of God's Word and applying them to your life).

3. *The outer life of Christian service* (expressing God's love through your concern for others).

Notice the word *cultivated.* A deep, lasting faith doesn't "just happen." It results from active cooperation with the Holy Spirit.

Mission: Possible

Daniel wasn't being a hero when he knelt by that open window. He was simply doing what he had done for many years as an act of devotion and loyalty to God.

If bad habits are hard to break, so are good habits. Daniel wasn't about to falter in this tough situation. His roots were too deeply imbedded in a love for God.

Most of us WANT to be good examples of Christianity, but we soon discover that SAYING we believe something is a lot easier than DOING it! We have good intentions, but

we give in to our feelings,

or think, *Next time I'll do better,*

or decide, *It doesn't really matter. Who will ever know?*

During a tournament, a pro golfer accidently hit the ball with his putter, causing it to rock very slightly. No one saw his action, but he reported it anyway. One point was deducted from his score. Although he lost the tournament by one point, he was not a "loser"! Honesty meant more to him than winning.

When habits take us away from God, rather than toward Him, it's time to make changes.

"You were taught . . . to put off your old self, which is being corrupted by its deceitful desires; to be made new in the attitude of your minds; and to put on the new self, created to be like God in true righteousness and holiness" (Ephesians 4:22-24, NIV).

This involves an exchange of values: ours for God's. At first, this is a real struggle. Again and again our values will be tested. In each situation we must decide: Will I go God's way, or choose another path? The decisions are never easy, but as we repeatedly seek to go God's way, a pattern begins to form. Our values become clearer—to ourselves and to others.

When we fail to live up to our beliefs, we experience guilt, a sense of worthlessness, and a tendency to quit trying or to deny our beliefs. The pattern of defeat, however, can be broken. Keep in mind that a life of victory is built on little things: a word here, a thought there—a continual moving in the direction of WANTING to please God and demonstrate love for Him.

"To Obey Is Better . . ."

While many people dislike the word *obedience*, the fact is, like Dylan sings, "You gotta serve somebody." It is to our advantage if that SOMEONE is God (Romans 6:16, 22).

"If you love me," Jesus said, "keep my commandments" (John 14:15). There is no way to separate obedience from the Christian life. And it is in the course of obedience that God meets us with His strength and we develop a fuller, firmer faith.

The force that makes this possible is the Holy Spirit, nudging us toward the right decisions, spotlighting the pattern of right action in God's Word, yet never taking away our freedom to choose.

The real test of our values comes in the wear and tear of daily experience: at school, home, and work. The first-century Christians, like Daniel, were ready to put their lives on the line—to be burned alive, eaten by wild animals, tortured to death—rather than surrender their faith in Christ. Their love for Him came before anything else.

How will you respond to life?
    to your family?
        to your environment and peers?
            to temptation?
                to troubles and tests?
                    to challenges and social change?
The answer lies in your values.
The choice is yours.

DISCOVERY PROJECT: CHARTING FOR CHANGE

1. List the changes you would like to make in your life within the next year. ______________________________

____

2. List the changes you think God would like you to make.

____

3. List one thing you can do to make an immediate change in your inner life. ______________________________

____

4. List one thing you can do to make an immediate change in your behavior or conduct. ________________

____

5. List one thing you can do on a daily basis to demonstrate your loyalty to God. ________________

____

P.S.

Now that you have studied about values, you may feel a sense of satisfaction. After all, you're a Christian, and proud of it! You're not afraid to stand for what you believe. You are making efforts to live the Kingdom life here and now, and you know this pleases the Lord.

Beware of a sneaky, silent, creeping disease: spiritual pride (sometimes known as self-righteousness). Right now, memorize the antidote!

1. *The best we can do can never earn salvation.* This comes as a gift from God, through the death and resurrection of Jesus Christ.

2. *We are debtors.* We owe everything we have to God.

3. *We are human.* Failures have been known to occur at all stages of life.

4. *There is only ONE perfect example:* Jesus Christ. Becoming like Him is a lifetime process.

5. *Any spiritual achievement is only possible through His divine aid.* He is our support system and lifeline throughout our stay on planet earth.

"Thine is the Kingdom, the power, and the glory," should be our prayer.

43